MW01048827

Zoom in on the PLEDGE OF ALLEGIANCE

Zoom in on American Symbols

Heather Moore Niver

E **Enslow Publishing**
101 W. 23rd Street
Suite 240
New York, NY 10011
USA

enslow.com

WORDS TO KNOW

allegiance Loyalty to a country or its leader.

immigrant A person living in a foreign country.

indivisible Cannot be divided or torn apart.

patriotism Strong feelings for a person's country.

pledge A serious promise.

recite To repeat from memory.

salute A special position that shows respect.

symbol An image or shape that stands for another thing.

unity To be a single part, or together as one.

CONTENTS

The Pledge of Allegiance began as a way to have flags in every public school. Today it is recited in many places by people of all ages.

The Original Pledge

All over the United States, many children start their school days in a similar way. They file into class. Their teacher takes attendance. And in many schools, students stand up to say the Pledge of Allegiance together.

Writing the Pledge

In August 1892, the United States was still recovering from the Civil War. Daniel Sharp Ford thought the country needed some unity. He thought it would help the nation's patriotism if every school had an American flag. He owned a magazine called the *Youth's Companion*. He thought that he could use his magazine to spread the word about flags.

Ford asked an author and minister named Francis Bellamy to write the Pledge of Allegiance. It would be a special pledge for the American flag. Bellamy hoped that American students would say it together, but he also hoped that any country could use it. The Pledge of

Thousands of copies of the *Youth's Companion* containing the Pledge of Allegiance were sent to classrooms across the United States.

Allegiance he wrote is a little different than the one we say today. Bellamy wrote: "I pledge allegiance to my Flag and the Republic for which it stands, one nation, indivisible, with liberty and justice for all." This pledge became the words that many Americans know by heart today.

Francis Bellamy wrote the first version of the Pledge of Allegiance.

Avon Public Library

Reciting and Saluting

Bellamy knew he needed some help getting the word out about the pledge. He asked the United States Congress to support a special ceremony. President Benjamin Harrison announced a holiday called Columbus Day. October 12, 1892, marked the 400th anniversary of Christopher Columbus landing in America. Millions of children recited the Pledge of Allegiance that day.

United States President Benjamin Harrison made Columbus Day a holiday. The Pledge of Allegiance was first recited on this day.

A schoolteacher leads her children in the pledge in 1942.

Soon reciting the pledge became a way that students in every public school started their day. In fact, Americans everywhere started to recite the Pledge of Allegiance together. They said it in campgrounds, at public meetings, or just about anywhere they saw an American flag.

The Bellamy Salute

People did not feel right just staring at the flag with their hands at their sides as they said the pledge. Luckily, the *Youth's Companion* included instructions for a special Bellamy salute. Everyone should reach their arm out straight in front of them and a little bit upward. For years, this was how people said the Pledge of Allegiance.

A Change in the Salute

The salute was changed during World War II (1939–1945). The United States was fighting against countries like Italy and Germany. The Bellamy salute was similar to one used by the Nazi Party in Germany. To make sure their own salute was different, on December 22, 1942, the United

The Bellamy salute was too much like the Nazi salute that these children are giving. It was changed to placing the hand over the heart.

The Nazi Party

The Nazi Party in Germany was responsible for the deaths of millions of people, like the Jewish people, just because of their religion.

States Congress declared that Americans should salute the flag with their hands over their hearts. This change shows how powerful a symbol like a salute can be.

Changes

The Pledge of Allegiance was a huge hit with Americans. But not everyone was happy with the pledge. Soon some changes were made.

Improvements to the Pledge

In 1923, some Americans got together and held the National Flag Conference. They decided that they could improve the words in the pledge. They voted to change "my flag" to "the

flag of the United States." They wanted to make sure immigrants to America knew they were saluting the US flag. In 1924, the second conference added "of America" to be more specific.

Immigrants look at the American flag. The words of the pledge were changed to make it just for the United States.

Adding "Under God"

Even though a minister wrote the Pledge of Allegiance, it did not refer to God until 1954. A religious group and some other people went to Congress and argued that the pledge should include the phrase "under God." They asked that it be included in the line with "one nation indivisible." President Dwight Eisenhower signed it into law on June 14, 1954.

Today some people feel that the nation's pledge should not refer to religion. Not everyone in the United States believes in God.

Fast Writing!
Frances Bellamy thought up and wrote the Pledge of Allegiance in only two hours!

Rules of the Pledge

Congress made the Pledge of Allegiance even more official in 1942, which was its fiftieth anniversary. The pledge itself was already important. Some states required public school students to begin each school day by reciting it. Congress created a code for the pledge. For example, people should stand, put their hands over their hearts, and take off their hats when saying it.

Schoolchildren say the pledge in the 1940s.

Hats Off!

Men can leave their hats on while reciting the Pledge of Allegiance if they are wearing them for religious reasons or for the military. People in the military should salute.

No Pledge Required

Not every American loved the Pledge of Allegiance. In 1943 the Supreme Court ruled that Americans had free speech, and so they should not be forced to say something, such as the Pledge of Allegiance.

Uniting the United States

The Pledge of Allegiance is an important American symbol. Reciting these lines together can unite many citizens of the United States. The Pledge of Allegiance recited today is: "I pledge allegiance to the flag of the United States of America, and to the republic for which it stands, one nation under God, indivisible, with liberty and justice for all."

Avon Public Library

The United States of America is not the only country to have a special way to honor their flag or country. Other countries are just as proud of their flag or country as Americans are. Use this research activity to find out more about the countries across the globe and how they salute their flag.

1. Using a globe, map, or atlas, pick four different countries from all different areas of the world. Draw a picture of your country or print out a picture from the internet.

2. Using the internet, atlas, or books in the library, look up information about each country. If you need help, ask a parent, teacher, or librarian to direct you to books or websites that will help you find this information.

3. Do these countries have flags? Draw a picture of each flag or print each one out from the internet.

4. Do these countries have a special pledge they say to their flag? If they do, write it down next to your picture or print it out.

5. If any of the countries do not have a pledge, how do they create a sense of patriotism? Look up information about whether they have a song, sometimes called an anthem, or other ways to feel unity with other people in their country. Write it down or print it out.

6. Combine your information for each country's flag, pledge, or songs.

4/17
j 323.6
N

LEARN MORE

Books

Harness, Cheryl. *Flags Over America: A Star-Spangled Story.* Chicago, IL: Albert Whitman & Company, 2014.

Mora, Pat. *I Pledge Allegiance.* New York, NY: Alfred A. Knopf, 2014.

Rustad, Martha E. H., and Kyle Poling. *Why Are There Stripes on the American Flag?* Minneapolis, MN: Millbrook Press, 2015.

Websites

Ben's Guide to the US Government

bensguide.gpo.gov/liberty-bell-1753/35-age-4/apprentice-symbols-of-us-government/86-pledge-of-allegiance-1892

Learn about American symbols, including the Pledge of Allegiance and more!

Social Studies for Kids

socialstudiesforkids.com/articles/ushistory/pledgeofallegiancehistory.htm

Get more facts about the Pledge of Allegiance.

INDEX

Published in 2017 by Enslow Publishing, LLC.
101 W. 23rd Street, Suite 240, New York, NY 10011

Copyright © 2017 by Enslow Publishing, LLC.

All rights reserved.

No part of this book may be reproduced by any means without the written permission of the publisher.

Cataloging-in-Publication Data

Names: Niver, Heather Moore.

Title: Zoom in on the Pledge of Allegiance / Heather Moore Niver.

Description: New York : Enslow Publishing, 2017 | Series: Zoom in on American symbols | Includes bibliographical references and index.

Identifiers: ISBN 9780766084384 (pbk.) | ISBN 9780766084407 (library bound) | ISBN 9780766084391 (6 pack)

Subjects: LCSH: Bellamy, Francis. Pledge of Allegiance to the Flag—Juvenile literature. | Flags—United States—Juvenile literature.

Classification: LCC JC346.N58 2017 | DDC 323.6'5—dc23

Printed in China

To Our Readers: We have done our best to make sure all website addresses in this book were active and appropriate when we went to press. However, the author and the publisher have no control over and assume no liability for the material available on those websites or on any websites they may link to. Any comments or suggestions can be sent by e-mail to customerservice@enslow.com.

Photos Credits: Cover, p. 1 (inset) Elyse Lewin/Photographer's Choice/Getty Images; cover, p. 1 (background flag) Stillfx/Shutterstock.com; p. 4 Christian Delbert/Shutterstock.com; p. 7 Library of Congress Prints and Photographs Division; p. 9 Stock Montage/Archive Photos/Getty Images; p. 10 Alfred Eisenstaedt/The LIFE Picture Collection/Getty Images; p. 12 Topical Press Agency/Hulton Archive/Getty Images; p. 15 Bettmann/Getty Images; p. 17 Education Images/ Universal Images Group/Getty Images; p. 19 Esther Bubley/The LIFE Images Collection/Getty Images; p. 20 Elsa/Getty Images; interior pages graphic elements amtitus/DigitalVision Vectors/Getty Images (flag page borders), funnybank/DigitalVision Vectors/Getty Images (flag in circle), hvostik/Shutterstock.com (hand over heart)